Regeneration White Book

Meirion Jordan

D0815392

SEREN

Seren is the book imprint of
Poetry Wales Press Ltd.
57 Nolton Street, Bridgend, Wales, CF31 3AE
www.serenbooks.com

ISBN: 978-1-85411-555-3

A CIP record for this title is available from the British Library.

The publisher acknowledges the financial assistance of the Welsh Books Council.

Cover art: Simon Hicks

Printed in Bembo by The Berforts Group Ltd, Stevenage

Contents

Preface   7

Part I

Prologue   13
1. Cei   17
2. Bedwyr   21
3. Owain   26
4. Gwalchmei   31

Part II

5. Gwenhwyfar   37
6. Drystan   41
7. Dinadan   45
8. Esyllt   49
9. Elen   53

Part III

10. Galaad   61
11. Melwas   66
12. Le chevalier mal fet   71
13. Medraut   76
Epilogue   81

Preface

Yet I woll nat say that hit shall be so; but rather I wolde sey,
here in thys worlde he chaunged hys lyff.

With these words Thomas Malory made his farewell to an ideal of king-
ship 'that was already largely in abeyance when they must have been
written. Certainly Arthur embodied it, and that he did so was no accident,
since the equation of Arthur's fortunes with those of the British people
was a literary idea at least three hundred years old when Malory began his
work. Malory, like so many before and after him who have written some-
thing like it, was placing a kind of Britain to rest with Arthur in his
uncertain tomb.

The central myth that ties the pieces of this book together is that of
regeneration, and the triangles of marriage that shape Malory's version –
Arthur, Launcelot, Gwenyver; Trystram, Mark, Isoud – seem to have at
their root the same concerns of issue and generation that bind Pwyll,
Rhiannon and Gwawl in the *Mabinogi*. It is in connection with this myth
that I conduct my interrogation of Arthur's world, and it is with this in
mind that I try to enmesh it in language; not simply to memorialise this
change of livings but to anticipate it and make it speak. So in particular I
interpret Arthur's death as a regenerative one, a tacit admission of the
future's possibility as much as it is a recognition of the past's value. I may
well be fortunate that, in setting out after Arthur in these terms, even the
slightest success may still be a success, though it is set about with failures
– a point that occurred to Malory, I suspect, centuries before it occurred
to me.

7

For the identity of Arthur is in some doubt here: certainly I do not enquire after it in the simplistic, historical terms of establishing a 'real' Arthur, since it is probably safe to say that such questions will never be answered with any certainty except in the minds of those who ask them, and wish for them to have answers. Rather I wish to explore how this attractive, romantic, fundamentally distant world of Arthur and his knights relates to the one we live in, and how the links between the inevitable demise of Arthur and our own farewells to whatever parts of our lives we are forced to leave in the past may be re-forged. This is no simple process, for the world of Arthur is fixed in time and we who are continually sliding forwards into the present are fortunate that it occasionally reaches out to snag some small details of who we are, or have been.

Perhaps that is too oblique. Where I have found some point of contact between the inevitable shape of Arthur's story and the shape of my own memories, I have tried to bring them together through annotation. These links between the overlapping worlds of the text – the personal margin and the entangling ground of literary tradition – are vital in the process of interrogation I mentioned above, and although by refusing to make the precise nature of this contact apparent I have left some of this interroga-tion to the reader, I suspect that too much precision would risk obscuring the reader's relation to Arthur in favour of my own. Fitting my own notes to the main text, in short, was my attempt to identify Arthur and bring a grief deeply felt but tenuously experienced to light: I have tried to leave room for the reader to do the same.

Equally, I have refused to allow Arthur's world to occupy its own over-bearing space in the poem, but have tied it as closely as I can to its expression in the works of the Arthurian tradition; and if I make use of certain obscure or archaic terms the reader will have to bear with me, though I have tried to avoid complete obscurity where possible. Therefore although the language I have used to frame Arthur is substantially modern – for if Arthur is alive anywhere in this writing he is alive now, in our terms - I have tried to keep Arthur within certain bounds, which these archaisms, borrowings, quotations and references attempt to mark out.

The story of Arthur, then, is firstly a valediction: Arthur must die, or at least depart; his life, which is the life he possesses from us, must change beyond recognition. It would not be a book of the death of Arthur other-wise, and here too the distant, alienated personae of Arthur's world attempt to reckon what they have lost in Arthur. This is the well-trodden ground of literary tradition, however, and I am only here to pace it out as far as I must, since the process of interrogating Arthur for the part of ourselves invested in him needs an aim beyond nostalgia and sentimental recollection. It is rather that by measuring out the length of Arthur's passage through my own history I am looking to give shape in my understanding to the lives he might yet live, the new versions which he will doubtless inhabit for other writers, other readers.

In light of all this, then, it would come as no surprise that for a hero destined to return and return again, for someone whose death is synonymous with their embarkation, Arthur's epitaph is as good as his genesis. And if I may be forgiven a small play upon its wording, I think it only right to begin:

HIC IACET ARTHURUS, REX QUONDAM REX FUTURUS.

Incipit liber mortis Arturi.

Part I

Prologue: Merlin

Arthur[1]

                              was my king:

before the names, the places where sunlight undifferentiated
              touched waters   I was the dream   I woke
              & that was a beginning,

                                   the north.

I was the saints, and the wild barley;
wood wose upon a time begging,

                                   until I found him. Through
              the vortex where the gods poured
              into a shape of the world;
              almond eyes sheer as the stone
              or whorled in La Tène pools;

                                   bearded, penned in by the palm,
                                   the palm. Rosette. Yet
I was before him, and after him, triskele.

              Without him, nothing.

I – ripple in the pool in which the heroes drank
the gods' knowledge, the well where those living dabbled
hands in the low-dark ocean of the dead
I – was before the names of the walls, border of lotus,
and the hills
      and the rivers – I

---

1. My grandfather died on the 18th of February, 2008, not quite 96 years old. It was
not a sudden or an unexpected death; he had been seriously ill for some time before
that, and by the end he was entirely bedridden. His brother had died a few years before
– who, with the possible exception of my grandmother – was closer to him than
anyone. By the end he had suffered several strokes and his recollection of most things
was poor. The only conversation he could make during the last years of his life mostly
concerned his boyhood in Pant, above Merthyr, in what must have been (by my reck-
oning) the 1920s.

knew him like my own,
shaped him, fathered him – by border of lotus –

on the pieces of Britain, which lodged piercing
in his too human heart. Britain was him

& Britain, wrenching with grief
the poor & rusted panels of his story

made him king.

What was he sum of? He

ebb-tide of the Caesars lapping
past Glevum, past Venta Icenorum,

attic fragments, Jupiter Ammon,
the memory of Maximianus and Constantine
drawing itself tall in the ashes. There I see him,
the head of Apollo with its grown – palm, palm! –
green-bronze hair still glimmering.

Arthur was king; but he was more
than the new-dug hoards laid
in September frost
and their shining;

far more than the carnyx
mouthing in the camps of Mars; [& in Arthur's face too
the boar opens its eyes]
nor truly – Jupiter Ammon but the horned
and unnamed one, Cernunnos cognate? Nor
Maponos – awesome inworld gaze! -
splitting sky like hoofbeats:

more, by those almond eyes,
he was Maglocunos, & Owain & Urien,
a watcher of coasts and safe harbours,
seafarer, Breton, the High-Queen's husband
& sometime lord;

and unhappy father, he who was all kings
before and after, 2
                 least happy of all;

& through his great Thames-fished shield the rust-green
pinpricks glimmer [among triskele, ripple, lofted palm] as stars.

I dreamed & in my dream
         [led by boar, the stag, the wild dog] under those ever
         dividing waters
                 Arthur was us,
                 and we, filling him like a cup
                 which, drawn, shows itself the void
                 between two faces staring,
                 not kissing, nor reconciled;
                 a hope never quite realised, or lost:

Arthur

                 was a trick of the light, he was

the long shadow
of his own name, & we behind him
were the flame, we in the mouth spitting
toothless into the fire, against the cold, or the murrain,
or the evil eye: we the fire and the mould and metal.

                 Arthur, brittle as wax.
                 My lost original of Britain.

And again it was the saints and the holy wells,
it was the sons of Llyr striding, or it was water-spirits,
a land of sees and sea-curbed monasteries
or genius loci, giants and undines,
                 of which Arthur was king;

---

2. In the photographs I have of him he is at somebody else's wedding: short, balding
even then, with thin black hair and glasses. Or forty years later on a deckchair at
Weston-Super-Mare. His brother is nearby in both pictures (in one he might even be
the groom) and they are smiling. In both pictures there are people I hardly recognise.

Britain it was, Britain it always was,
in the tides, and the surf raking
back blood from shore
to shingled shore:

he, on his dark hill. The grave-mouth beckoned
    & sun burned its spirals on the sky;
    the mess of bones were chivalry,

        the mound: calvary's gift;[3]

or king of his hall, and the reeked turf, and a few hills
and sodden ground, showing his hearth's honour

      in the cutting of hair;

always of Britain, he was our king;

where before *imrannán*, islands. Before the wedding,
the land. Crowned: the ringed stones fencing sky;
always of Britain, and his own heart breaking:[4]

Arthur was Britain, Arthur my king.

3. Many of his stories I can only recall imperfectly – of piano lessons, struggling to play Swannee River which his brother had long ago mastered, of cycling down the steep hill from Dowlais, of the teachers in Cyfartha school – but I think of Emma Calvé singing the same tune my grandfather would occasionally hum, and the words he would never quite let go. Wireless. Gramophone. Robeson and others singing in his sitting-room.
4. I wish I remembered more of my grandfather's anecdotes with any kind of clarity, but he taught O and A level English for thirty years. He taught Chaucer and the poems of Christina Rossetti, along with Shakespeare and the Romantics. He would often recite lines from poems he once knew by heart, but had forgotten.

1. Cei

I remember the year they killed Uther,
blood bells among the heather.
Pendragon. Pen draig oedd arnaw.

Too soon.[5] Ambrosius, Uther, and the main act.
I call a rule of three & three times three:
kings, weapons, companions;
Arthur, his sword and me.

So,

                where was he? Truth,

I was the first: the first piece that went
to the making of Britain; Cei hir,

        taller than the tallest tree of the forest,
        my sword mortal in its maiming,

        stronger than any of the Coeling,
        than Dalldaf ap Cunyn Cof,
        than Moren ap Iaen,
        and all the men from Dyffryn Conwy;

           my gestures call them:
           magicians and giants[6]

---

5. I may not be incidental to this narrative. I am very different from the people of my grandfather's generation: educated in Welsh up to the age of eight, then sent to a private school in Swansea, then to Oxford, I have a tendency to overshoot my meanings, from which perhaps incident, incoming at an improbable speed.

6. One story my grandfather mentioned to me once was of the local boys plaguing a local widow who they called Betsy Cwmanod, who I think lived in Cwmanod cottage outside Llanddew, beside the Onddu. My grandfather even remembered the song they sung at her, but apart from her name it seems to be nonsense – much like his distantly remembered version of Calon Lân. I have sometimes wondered what Betsy Cwmanod was like, and why the local boys teased her, but perhaps they needed no other reason than that she was old, and lived alone.

I tell you, I was the first,
and gave my all for Arthur.

Upon a time. Once:

was only a child, a weak thing struggling to be,
grasping the threads of his own story
as though fighting for breath. Twice:

a boy, a blink of an eye
a man, a rider, a prince
in his father's kingdom: famous

shield-shearer, gift-giver, a wall
to his hearth and household,
but still a man. That was the Arthur

that could grow old, and huddle
toothless in winter, gobbing
at embers; among dung, and dogs,

and his unweaned brats. Three times:

that is a small fire; that is a boy
who will be a man who will be
                    Pendragon now   and once again.

            Another king; a golden rule:
            in your own tale you play the fool.

So surly and dog-faced slouching
I made Arthur staring with wonder,
the young man
                    on his horse, riding

            To Coed Celyddon, to Badon,
            to Gaul, to Joyous Guard
                    and Camlann,

bitter Camlann
        and Avalon
            and the dark barge turning out to sea.

Arthur, forgive me.
      Forgive me.

I remember the year that they killed Uther.
Blood on the heather. The ravens who gnaw.
                Who knows

if it was Saxons
or men of Dal Riada,
for Britain was now and long-ago
when I was first, and gave for Arthur.[7]

Arthur

           was king, but not yet king;

& all the years after,
when I was a churl, when the price of the story
was a stone on his chest,
& gold rings, & the wind breathing
through a cairn's mouth:

      his heartbreak, betrayal,
      and the white isle, immortal;
      I knew him; the boy Arthur.

7. Then there was his strange amusement at being greeted by somebody – in the mid-thirties now I think – by a very ordinary call of 'shwmae', which he thought should be followed (in his own words) 'shwdichieri'. I can remember him telling me with some pride what they meant, in spite of the fact that I already knew (at the age of ten, and again at the age of twelve, and so on). 'How are you?', 'How are you today?'

Not yet a man, not yet my foster-brother,
not yet quite sprited
from the walls of Tintagel;

not Britain yet, still he was Arthur.

I was the first, the first given and passed over.
Happy child, in the year they killed Uther
        a boyhood was only the first out of three:

first deeds; who would follow his father
as king of his hills, and his moors, and his heather,
        hunting deer and hare along dyffryn Teifi,

who would grow old, and suffer,
careworn and bitter.
                                        Arthur,[8]

                        Arthur, forgive me.

8. That world constantly slips my mind: Pant and Vaynor, with the train up to Pontsticyll
and Torypantau and its tunnel, then down seven-mile bank to Tal-y-bont and Brecon
– for his father worked for a time on the railway yards at Merthyr, so he remembered
a great deal about that vanished world of the trains running 'five and six times down
to Dowlais, five and six times back the same way,' from Welsh to English and back again.

2.Bedwyr

Alone of all his knights, I knew:
Arthur gathered from doubtful, circumscribed
or nonexistent sources, drawn remarkably

into the light;

> Walter the   archdeacon
> with his   eloquent,
> expedient   book;

Igraine his mother, Morgana and Morgause
his half-sisters of Orkney.

I was his cupbearer, perhaps his seneschal.
It seemed like a story I'd heard
                 somewhere before.[9]

Arthur, as I knew him

                           was the union
of houses, the flow and counterflow of styles
down a margin's leaf. First scribe – his mother's side –

                the old half-darkness,

the islesmen in their warcoats ganging
from Hebrides to kirk-stone relief,
                 the broch-dwelling people

9.After leaving school, he taught, as he would for almost sixty more years. He went to University in Cardiff in 1933, after which he resumed teaching. He rarely mentioned those years directly, so I sometimes have to interpolate other material: in that year King Kong was first shown, the singing telegram was invented, Cambridge won the boat race, and Everton and Manchester City wore association football's first numbered shirts for the final of the FA cup.

of their forts and crowning-stones made

a kind of magic: to see in a stone house, low
as a boat the whorls and circles
of a high cross. Second scribe, perhaps his father:

Caroline minuscule. Most telling
in the consistently abbreviated
Imperator
Dux Bellorum
but more, the need to write in full:
vexillum proponendum; senatus populusque,
but a poor copy: Charlemagne's legal codes
shot through with dog-latin. So

by his vanishing
from night-walled Tintagel, we have the curious juxtaposition:
marginally, the changeling; yet fol. 1ʳ gives the saviour's image
driven to barbarous Egypt, somewhere
between orthodoxy and heterodoxia:

without a vulgate to break his fall.[10]

Poor child. But these, they were

the years of his great triumph.
Germane to Constantine's throne

as they – convenient thousands of them – swarmed
through Gaul I exulted in him,
and being near him. Arthur was king

of the Romans and Britons, inheritor of tributes
beyond the measure of his ill-recorded age:

hardly a twilight, except for the few clear stars;

10. And other events: Talybont resevoir was completed in 1938, displacing around 200
people. The Brecon and Methyr Railway was closed in 1964, with the army demolish-
ing Torypantau station. By this time, my mother was growing up in Grays in Essex
among (largely Welsh) teaching families where she was not allowed to watch the new
television serial, Doctor Who.

Britain kicking back sand from backwash
to backwash, from cusp to cusp
of the new histories

which were much as the old,
the well-attested,

                    the coming of the Saxons.

Arthur

              was our strong tower

in those years, in whose foundation
the cave remained. And Morgause

              was our queen, the favoured of Arthur,
              in his wars of the north; against Gorre

and Gododdin, Dumbarton and Dal Riada;
where in bas-relief they rush headlong, history
against legend, Brython and Barbarian,

kin against kin. And lying with him,
with the magic fretted
              in the whorls of her hair:

She knew,   as I did,
      Geasa   against   *Logos*
       word   against   *bond*

              of that night-
              tangling came
              the ruin of Britain.

Black water shelves from the oar. Arthur I have dreamed

of your *imrannán,* the one journey
where none followed you: [11]

Cold Prydwen sloughing west-oceans
from her prow;

Arthur in his small boat drifting
into history, to return
            as Arthur *locutor,* the hero.

Arthur   they are closing iron doors behind you
as you go slowly

to the land of the dead,   as you are crossing the dark
and storm-shifted beach
                        of the other world.

Arthur I have dreamed of empty mouths
            lining the far walls of cloud. Peiriau,

they say: where the world floats
in a cauldron's eye.

The sea
            mutters its holy numbers, threes
                and sevens. Returning you are carried over.

Then Pen-cawr, Pen Iwerddon, Arthur you are rumoured in that
                                            slight
        rain that precedes all history
                                to be drifting
between nameless shores.   Behind the cliff-shadow aghast
            with storms the island
        of the mighty and the fair.

---

11. What did they do during the war? It was a familiar question then. My paternal
grandfather flew Lancasters in the coastal command. My great-uncle on my mother's
side was a conscientious objector, and so fabricated machine parts for mass production:
I'm told he walked to Coventry overnight after it had been bombed to find my great-
aunt. My other grandfather suffered a breakdown whilst serving as an army clerk.
Nobody seems sure what happened. I remember him telling me never to join the army.

In dreams I have sieved   from the round cromnen
        of beat-bronze
                the doom of Britain,

        where you pull yet, without me, on those in-world tides.
                You return and yet do not return.[12]

Poor child. Poor Arthur,

                        who would have killed his son,
                shame, shame:

what links a treasure
and a marriage?

                        Gold being the child of gods:
the ruin of Britain had a name.

12. Like everyone else, as best they could, they went back to their lives. My father's father went back to work on the fish dock in Hull, my great-uncle went on as a metal-work and mathematics teacher. My other grandfather met my grandmother at a school in Grays, in Essex. They holidayed at Bournemouth, Swannage, Southend.

3. Owain

A beheading game. A feast. Arthur
        against his court a crowned daub:

                cracks in him fine as the flaking
    of gold leaf. Dead men fresh in their graves.
    The cauldron simmered
        with their voices, ours.

Christ the Redeemer stands ensign
      over the ranked shrouds. What boy
      brings news of the heavenly kingdom?
        A small fault being token
          of a great flaw.

Green: verdure; lost, ancient woods that hold houses,
           recluse behind walls, as pearls
              in washed silk;
        colour of evil, imp-gall, tests of rectitude;
        thereafter envy, and the knight stands
         by board

snubbing the porters and magnates, the lords, ladies, squires
    as the wonder passes, and the hall shakes in the wind.[13]

In all this Arthur sat quiet. Gwenhwyfar moving
about the tables was grace in a bright room.

I, like the rest: I loved her. No knight
who caught her eye, as she brought them the cup

went unscathed. These were
the high days of Arthur,

---

13 Little Belmore, above Church Stretton on the Long Mynd in Shropshire, is another point of contact. My mother would spend her summer holidays there with her cousins and her grandmother. Until it was badly rebuilt in the 1970s, it retained its original shape: an old, whitewashed longhouse fishing at the springline. From the top of the Long Mynd, you can see the hills of Powys beyond Bishop's Castle and Wentnor, on a clear day.

the bright rebirth, without hint
of the dead lord's goblet, or the sisters:

      Morgana, Elene, Morgause.
      My mother, my kin;

                    I had my part

in Arthur's ruin.

Green: Urien my father, Urien Fawr,
Urien of Rheged and of Gorre,
pride of the north, shield of the Kynveirchin
        (and the tides sweep their blood from shore to shore);

withdrawn from the south, from the ash-mantled
fossa and banks
          of well-walled Caerleon,

they sent no mischief, no poisoned wedding-gift
but they sent sons.

      Gwalchmei the fairest,
      Gaheris his shield-bearer,

              and me, dwyrain ffosawd.

Still in my heart, I knew Arthur[14] –
playing gwyddbwyll at evening
among fair-headed lads –

      Arthur dwelt ever   on his wife's dowry,
      the round table   and its hundred earls
      his royal thought   wandering. A green stain

---

14. It is an out-of-the-way place, even now. Their nearest neighour was Jones the
Hollows, who tried to warm his bathwater by wrapping the bottom of the tub in a
wire heating element, only to burn himself on the hot metal. His television was
powered directly by windmill for a time, and the family would cluster round the set
whose picture grew and shrank in time with the wind.

on gold and enamel is what? Mirabilia arc earthward,
          Arthur in his dais-siege channeling
between Usk-bank and heaven.
                                                    What can I say?
We were proud,
Orkneyings of the Out Isles,
harnessed and girt for the assault;

                              We were not ready
                              for the king of a forest country
                              and his young queen

breaking the hall doors open
with the burning of lamps.
Then brent the rafter-timbers with bright gold
and their welcome;
                              We were not ready
                              to meet Arthur
                              and love him.

Arthur

                              was our lord, and true,
                              in our quarrels, our timely murders;

                              we who loved Arthur
                              were his end and ruin.

I was beardless then; dressed like my brothers
at the five virtuous points,
                    indistinguishable
from the saddles and harness,
the hawk-and-brachet boors
that history sketched behind us.

Much was beginning to fade:
Merlin into the caves and woods
of Celydon, or Cornwall; the old heroes
into the tangles of duns and rivalries,

the slow wash of names leaking
with the ebb tide. Britain remained;

and we too lingered, passed
into stories, from tongue to tongue,[15]

shore to distant shore. Some
gathered storm-force: Gwalchmei my cousin
was one;

others being ripples skirting
the far holms and bays. Glewlwyd Gafaelfawr,
Selyf ap Sinoid, Gweir ap Gwestyl,
Mabon ap Modron,

only Arthur remembers them.

Arthur

was the cup that held us,

the deep well   and memory
of the western men,
through whom we too,
we flawed and faithless – penitent
on the cold floors at Christmas,
harbouring our faults
like an axe cleaving a rotten tree – we

who could still be drawn, as now,
through all those bitter years – I weep for them,
and for him,

15. I have only visited the house on Long Mynd once. My mother remains attached to
it as somewhere valuable from her childhood: she can remember clearly the trains from
Church Stretton to Bishop's Castle that she took in the sixties. Once, at the end of
summer, when it was time to leave again, she locked herself in the bathroom there.

who endured Camlann,
                    bitter Camlann,
          and the white sails shifting past the world's rim.

But it was Pentecost, Christmas, Easter, o gloria –
                    and the high day's hale
they drank at every seat of Arthur's hall.
Gwalchmei with his meat at table
          so that the ruin of Britain

might begin: begging that first adventure
          of his uncle, the king,[16]

                    where the wound is made – deeply –
                         and the axe-fall rings,

                    Arthur I loved beyond any man living,
                    though he was kin;

                    Arthur my beloved,
                    in prime, of great worship,
                    gentle and merciful
                              Arthur,

I betrayed him.

16. Nearby is the hillfort of Caer Caradog. You can walk there from Bishop's Castle without much difficulty, though I can remember being told of a shambolic expedition in the Bentley of a rich uncle to have a picnic on its summit. Some, like my grand-father and my great-uncle, were perhaps too eager to climb whilst others were too reluctant. It was sunny, though not everybody reached the top of the hill.

4.Gwalchmei

When I remember, the days
out of the darkness,
the shifting cloud-shadows
of the Out Isles:

       my mother and her sisters,
       the bold queens,
       the terrible,
       fair;

when I remember,
I remember Arthur.

          In the mind's eye the flush
          of barley-fringed islands,
          pollen flecks in the spring flood:

unbearable. Britain with its green overgrown
castrums, its tracked forests, the bluebells
overrunning ditch-works and dykes,

       the old sunken ways between byres
       set in rain-eaten ring-forts,

       and the fortified headlands
       defiant of the sea-peoples
       and their ships.

It was my land. It was not theirs.
Arthur our king welcoming Franks
and Saxons, Northmen and Romans:
             I felt the black mouths open in my heart.

I felt the deep unspeakable longing
that was the ground, that was the wood and water,
and the stone rood where the wind scrapes
Europe to a needle point: north.

> Peir dadeni, cauldron with your strange
> and holy power. I will be great! Christ
> > stay not my hand.[17]
> The magic wakes me. I killed green knights,
> > > red knights, blue.

> I killed my mother
> and my shadow grew.

When I remember, I
feel only the rush of horses
to the battle-front, the deep stone
stillness of the earth;
> > the blood letting on either hand.

Arthur
> was my king,

Arthur horned-head and intricate charging
field to banner field, upset against lion
or dragon rampant, Arthur my uncle
shouting over the battle-din:
> > > "to me, Gawain, to me"

> at bitter Camlann
> where I failed him.

Mother,

> I failed. Leave me alone;

17. My Mother's cousin, Norma, – the daughter of my grandfather's brother – was an
only child and my mother's best friend. Like my mother, she trained as a doctor and
they travelled in Europe together. We still, somewhere, have the camera she carried
with her to take the few odd pictures of Norway that sometimes turn up amongst the
unordered weddings and babies and family outings.

and the shingle cuts the tide from bone to bone,
from cliff to cliff.

I remember Ystrad Clyd, and Manaw,
and the small boats brinking

on the sea-smell;[18]

I remember well the sea-folk
ransacking legend and storehouse;

I remember Arfderydd, and Argoed Llwyfain,
and the days when we said: Arthur, the king,

will come again.

Mother and Arthur,
mistress and knight
in the cup of souls, embroidered
couchant, among barry-wavy
azure and argent,
as the barge turns slowly out to sea.
Mother, I beg you,

Leave me.

Don't leave me. It isn't time

not yet, to go back,
down to the saint-washed shore.

My brothers, my kin:

18. There are still a few photographs of her, looking just a little like my mother: on walking holidays in Switzerland, or hiking in Austria. She doesn't appear much alongside the rest of the family, but instead has her own separate enclave in their memories. She seems fenced-off, difficult to know. Then there are photographs that must be hers in which she never appeared, just as the dusty places at the back of my parents' cupboards sometimes give up her old things.

in the deep press of the battle I slept
and none woke me,

until the white gulls wheeling in
brought me

to the green apple islands
of my home.

My brothers, I beg you

greet me. Gareth my brother

why are you silent? What place is this? Mordred,
answer me,
whose bark is that
tipping and bobbing
in the calm bay?
Whose are the white sails, and the saints attending
dipping birds' eggs in the rain's shadow?

whose journey is it, that goes
on a wind charmed straight
as a swung line
beyond the storm's edge,

what stars can they look by,
what weathers will they find

when those far sands beach them?[19]

Oh mother, oh Arthur,

they are mine.

Explicit prima pars.

19. Norma died of cancer in 1987. She is the closest my parents' generation has to a
tragedy: small, subtle avoidances have accumulated around her, the faint smell of might-
have-been, the eagerly awaited futures that somehow never arrived. It is strange to
think of just what my mother missed in her.

Part II

5. Gwenhwyfar

If I understood him ever,
me, the Welsh girl with her head turned
by Norman patter,[20]

Arthur

           was my friend,

a kind man out of season
with the world. He was

like a mirror: full of your best ideas
about yourself, too bright and vivid
for the touch. Sequestered centuries

out of time, he woke me
to hounds calling
from the tapestry wood,

to Camelot, his house
of cold dreams:

                  the hearth blazed at Christmas,
                  the wind balustered and foined

          the Roman brick. Arthur at mass
          colder than the flags, cold enough
          to burn skin from careless,
                        supplicant hands;
the communion grail blazed
                in his sick glare.

---

20. My mother's mother, and her family, came from Shropshire. My grandmother grew up around Colebrookedale and Ironbridge, which she would cross each morning to go to school. Like my grandfather she became a teacher, first at a school for girls in Newport, just a few miles the other side of Telford, but not long after the war she moved away to teach in Essex, where she met my grandfather.

Therewith, a sennet: I, who followed every inch
and scrip of knighthood, in its hauberks tobrast,

its blazon and disguise
                    could never believe a word.

In the rasing off of helms,
the fewtered spears that broke armour,
                    cracked bone, stove spines and shields,

I could not abide. Nor the *gall-gael* kin of his, whose quiet,
factional murder – in the medleys by list and forest-eave,

in the flow of cloud and thunderhead from islands

                    far
                              to the west –

          spoke red volumes whose frets
          and counterpoint of carpet against word,

serpent enmeshing lion, dragon swallowed by dragon

it was like hearing your own language
as a dead tongue.

                                             And yet,
          and yet.

No, I won't talk of him. It is too much,

the flawed knight pondering
up and down the empty,
blasted land; [21]

the adulterers,

21. It is difficult at the distance of more than fifty years to make out just how they met,
and how they eventually married. I have only heard the story told once, not long, I
think, before my grandfather died. My grandmother was a keen tennis player in those
days, and on one particular day my grandfather's regular tennis partner was somehow
unavailable so my grandmother agreed to join him instead.

Jesu preserve me. Arthur

was the one man

I couldn't bear to hurt, and whose deep

cold

cauldron of a body
I could not love.

Such masculine oratory: my lady,
I prithee;

for it is you I love best[22]

after the chase, and hounds, and courtly wars.

Bob then. Wheel. On the rim
of the vessel the figures step
their antic carol. Dadeni

the water between them.

Knights, kneel. Yield you to me.
Who sent you?   Dadeni
a mass of arms
and harness in the pool.
A gift from that one broken knight.

Not yet. Please.

Not yet. Whose name
is like a wound to me,

---

22. I like to think that their domestic life was uncomplicated. There are still pieces of
furniture here and there which were originally bought for their house in Essex, just as
there are still outdated electrical appliances and scraps of carpet bought for their retire-
ment in Brecon on the hill above the old railway. Perhaps they will always be
un-remarkable, comfortable people when seen through their cheap utility furniture,
their old veneer-and-glass cabinet of small ornaments, trinkets, and a few photographs.

when in the years after

they called me Rosamund,
the shadow on their rich livings,

                          beautiful,
                          vernacular.

Arthur

      was nothing without me,
      a whorl,
      a shell,

whose vortex churned the blood from swell to swell, and drew
chivalry's driftwood behind.
                    Those bright, kind boys.
                    Owain, Gareth, Cei: heroes of tides

which turned; whose generations in their time were washed away.
Arthur,

      I have paid.
      I will pay.

But: I would do it again,

to see the one knight cross
that frost-heaved plain, the crippled king
whose caved groin wearies the earth,
as the legend's castle, with its spear and cup
fall slowly behind;

                  to see the knight
journeying onwards, step by ill-made step,

                       toward rebirth.

6. Drystan

One stone
can be a kingdom
under the sea:

       the flooded lanes,
       the steady knock of bells
       calling the drowned to prayer;

ah, the knife in my heart. Arthur

                     was the one

to call me, over the strand's half-cubits
of breaking surf, into his breathing dream

of Britain, its propriety, its manors beset[23]
by still-toothed wild.

Like him,
I had been nothing, a name
among the lich-mounds
whose soil crumbled black
              to show the crowns,
              the rings of crooked teeth. Such a man

my uncle was, desiring his champion
over the sea-lanes to Munster,

Dublin with its cargo
of bearded jarls. Such a man,
well versed in the salt-and-knife barter
of the sea-road. Forget him, said Arthur.

23. A generation beyond, my grandmother's father was a gamekeeper on the Walcot estate, where Robert Clive wrote 'Plassey' on the hillside in spruce. It is far enough back for me to be confused over just how everyone was related: somewhere there is a grandmother breeding gun-dogs and selling them to the Tsar of Russia, somewhere else an artillery horse-handler in the great war. Many seem to have died young.

Instead I donned helm and maunches,
cantered out
into chancery-field

to meet mine enemies, knights traitorous,
sans pité, Britain with the plague-pits reeking
of quicklime and psaltery. In my defiance

of that anointed right, I knew
it was the beginning of the end,

though the palfreys clattered still
over open fields, though Kernow and Dyfneint splendoured
in their vernacular prayer.

Call them, Arthur,

               let me see them again,

in the deep brambled life
between Lundy
and the blessed isles. Call her,

let me see her,
               fairer
than Gwennore,
the one worth kingdoms

                       though they lie under the sea.

And so it was, ware ever
of mine uncle's treachery, we came

to Logris and its bright kirtling waves,
where by grace, and worship

                    of that one foundered knight

      we won to a castle
of doomed loves, hight

Joyous Guard. Sometimes

the tale ends there,[24] as harpers have it:

my lords Lancaster and York,
a dragon gules preying on a boar passant argent;

the victory won, a history ushered to its close.

But at what price, those serjants thrown down
endlong and overthwart, unnamed from Penfro,

from Cantref Bychan, Guent Is-coed,
Gwynedd Uwch Conwy? Logris lying pacified

in a bushment, ever ready with its rocks and tides ground

to misericorde points,
ever with its supine teeth according
saracen, jew and paynim
with the hackbut's crackle. Arthur

amongst the foliage was at his height
as the sainted sixth, the lineal seventh,

brother to mismatched, corpulent eighth –

yet living in the fine timbers
of the minor gentry,[25] bordered
with sweet streams.

24. Inheritance has often been a temperamental process from that side of my family.
I can remember my mother telling me about a pair of candlesticks made from silver
sword-hilts of Prussian officers that went astray. And there are odd treasures we have
acquired too, such as the clock that was made and engraved for the beadle of a
Birmingham workhouse. My mother being a link through which many branches of my
family have passed their cast-off goods.
25. Was it very different, after years away to come back, not to Stieper Stones and
Wentnor but to Fan Big, Fan Nedd, Fan Gyhirich? From their house in Brecon my
grandmother could walk up Pen-y-Fan and back in a day, when they were still able; to
the saddle above Tal-y-Bont or to the edge of Llangors lake.

There too is the silhouette
of a breeze hung out
on a virginal sail,

below it the legend:
love potions, adultery,

my own unrecognised face
flying above a forest
of grotesques.

In a chapel
hard by the waves
I call on him,
my strong vessel,
my ark.[26]Arthur,

when at the last all failed,

when the black sails lifted in my mind
I will recall the one bond
that holds,

the one ship
that no lance,
no nail could sink;

Arthur
over the waters,
from Logris
to the islands
in that blessed sea
I beg you:

carry me.

---

26. Perhaps it was no return at all. Generations of one quarter of my family might be
buried in the churchyard at Cantref, a short walk away from Brecon; but the Baileys
are scattered across Shropshire and the midlands, from Shrewsbury to London.

7. Dinadan

So close I could almost
                    feel its breath
                    through the brast mails,

my destrier. A lover I

of the fingers' quick fluting down giterne strings,
the plays of love and miracle,
                              and maistrie,

after the good knights their fool
                              cantered I.

Having none ado with that, their ladies,
nor errant violence that left many unshriven
            torn through by the truncheon of a spear,

or the old trip, by way of Palomides, Damietta,
        Joseph of Arimethie[27] bearing responsibility

                    home. Arthur

was my fellow, laughing
with his fool's eyes;
                    doubtless

I did many fulsome deeds
by lane- and heath-side

                    but it was fellowship of knights
                    beseemed me best.

What is this place, exactly? The estates crumbled,

---

27. These other strangers; my father's family, the Jordans. My father was the first gen-
eration to live away from the fish-dock in Hull. My grandfather who sold fish and my
great-grandfather who caught it. I am tempted to call it a wandering name.

the saints and fables struck[28]

> faceless, and late summer
> bonfired of screens and altar-rails?

I have seen the aftermath
of a world of visions. The men gone
guardedly to church, their dutch-printed word
proudest in their grip.

> Arthur, my fool king,
> be merry; the best knight

of all the world rides with you. Ah,
among the wreckage the body
of my defaced saviour, of what
torn, passionate,
>> sweet muscles and wounds;
I would that best knight knew thee,
as he in woman's guise would send me
> hurtling to earth.

> A goodly knight of my hands,
> which I take to mean: hende

with kitchen-maids and stable-boys equally,

> mindful of a sharp verse
> in an inn's upper chambers,

Morfudd fel yr haul or somesuch somesuch;

> among the summer laundes, Arthur persists.

---

28. I try sometimes to peer into their world, but it is somewhere I know only second-hand. My father's parents, my other grandparents, both died of cancer almost twenty years apart: in my memory of my father's father I am holding a toy helicopter and my father is talking to his parents on a hill in the sunshine. In my next memory of them he is gone.

Arthur,

   I forgive you the knife
   between my ribs,

   your kin's aspersions,
   and the wounds they gave

   'through the thick of the thigh,'
   which is to say
       castrating me. Arthur,

     I am a fool
     and must forgive;

   the pride, lapses of memory; I
   as a fool forgive only
       for your fellowship –

and for the fellowship of the two knights
who above all others
      were the very flower;
   and for poor Lamorak, his face
   split bloody
      for a headless queen.

And other kindred riding

    by twos
      and threes

   Launceston to Ludlow,
   Durham to Dunstaffnage

    by our lady and all weathers: [29]

a pun, a riddle;

29. My father told me of how one summer holiday in the sixties he joined a friend's cousin, Eddie, delivering fish in his van over the East Riding, for the trade in small and unlikely catches. Gurnard, Halibut, Hake; Grimsby, Mablethorpe, Goole, I try to picture him lifting the boxes of fish and ice while his friend prevaricated, unwilling to join him in the work.

a sighting of small boats
as the MacDonald,
      as John des Isles

      take final bows

and Prydwen, cold with its hero sloughs

tide upon tide, wave on raking
wave, from Camlann,
        bitter Camlann,

to the island of apples,
and the stone-made lowes of saints,
   of my many;
        the lost loves;
much as came the Church-Dove
   out of Ireland. Arthur

      was at late summer, & the grass was green,
      fringing with yellow. The table was ready
      & the seats were full. It was a good time

     for Arthur,
        poor Arthur,
my king,
the fool:

after,

   when we were spent, with his head
   falling to the side, his eyes rolling,

   I put my ear to the brast mails
     as his breath, ragged,
      heaved from him. I wept,[30]

Lord, how I wept,
     my destrier.

---

30. My grandmother died remotely. My father travelled constantly from Glamorgan to Yorkshire to visit her through her long illness. I hold this space for them.

8. Esyllt

As the French book rehearseth,
    it was hard for me:

I saw the look in my king's eyes
    and knew it was over.

And even if I proved
    a rehearsal
before the main event,
    it was still my heart
that with every stroke of the sword,
    each discharge
of the ribaults
    blent.
          Fitzalan, Percy,
            Howard,

their falls and rises slipping like the high tide,
over the forgotten realm,
            that Britain —

    or was it Lyonesse? In either case

I think of the drowned,
of Llyr's spree stringing
from Shetland to Skellig,
    the young men hung
    by halters of Kelpie-hair,

    green, bloated and beautiful: Philip, thou paynim,
                never will you get worship mo;
    your soldiers have conquered a land that lies
        under the sea.
And as the book maketh mention,
    him I loved best, in his gentle masteries:

    the harp, the hawk,
    the soft words spoken
    over a cup's edge;

was no defence but Arthur. [31]

They did not understand
how the King of Ireland's daughter

was mistress of waves,
the night gales woken
in the mind's cup:

poor Arthur, his masculine romance
wearing its horns

proud as any bull; even I
who cared for them, Tristan
and Mark, Arthur
and his unnamed champion;

I charmed the waters
under their guileless feet.

When it was done, the same
facades remained:

parade armour, knightly effigy,
Mark the broken king

drifting step
by step
into feudal twilight. I wish

there could have been another way,
but save with broken hearts you cannot win

a queen of waves;

31. I am involved with history: these footnotes become harder to write. I was born in Morriston hospital, Swansea. I was educated in Welsh not only at the local primary school but at the Sunday school of the village's independent chapel where Welsh is still the language of religion. You must bear this in mind when I speak to you.

Christ is no saviour[32]
for those big-boned prelates
when houses slide whole

under a wrack of weeds.

When it was over,
with the lance twisted

between the ribbed muscle
of my man's heart,

then the surf rose black
in the bay's mouth,
wide as a galley, deep as a sail,
    as if to say:

western daughter,

            be calm.

There is a storm

        that will carry you away[33]

to your father, the king

        beyond the sea.

            Quiet. You

                are sinking

32. I remember the chapel. Old people clustering in the main pews, overlooked by empty galleries, singing hymns written by a brilliant few generations who are now beyond two generations in the past. And I have visited with choirs of old men who practice in workingmens' halls, in villages clinging to the edge of moorland. I cannot dismiss them, or my fleeting contact with them. I can neither leave or return to them. 33. Why would I mention them? They are still here, in a world which neither believes what they were brought up to believe, nor speaks the language that articulated them. I cannot articulate it. I am worried that I barely understand it.

you are floating

    further, from the air

you breathe:

        rest now −

but I did not, Arthur,
and I felt the sea working its heraldry,
        its pedigrees of rock and kelp

over me, per pale
            ten, twelve gouttes of
    breath,
            my breath.[34] Arthur

            was the sound of it,
            breaking surface

        in the long-ago,

        Logria,
    Lyonesse;

    my breath, my Britain,
    though it was black sails and poison, always
            it was Arthur

between sharp cliffs, below sea-chapels; by now the sound
    of dead souls coming up for air.

34. I cannot help but feel that these people, their expectations and beliefs, have been somehow betrayed. I see their struggles as though over my shoulder, or through a rear-view mirror; in dreams I am always driving away from them.

9. Elen

Descended by some tantalizing close degree
from near-neighbours of the tree of Jesse
a woman has a choice: but I
      let my guides be God and destiny.

Sweet Christ, my Lord. I have heard
      the tuckets and the din

           of Mordred's soldiers
           marching
               via Roundway and Raglan,

   the dim thunder of the cannon –

                 it calls for you, champion.

      By his glamoured eyes
      he was the only man for me;

         who made me vessel
         for the perfect one,

            the stainless knight steering
            over the womb's sea.

Black barge,
cog, coaster, holk:[35]

      from Knab to Nore, in his riding,
      shingle to dunes and the clear sky,
      shore to desolate shore,   he was the unmaking

          of Arthur.
If I'd known,

35. It was my parents who lived through my childhood in a small village at the very far end of the coalfield: they lived in Cardiff before I was born, on Rhumney Street, before they moved out to the very verges of Welsh Wales. A mile or so from my house the rivers begin to run west into the Loughor and Ystrad Tywi.

I wouldn't have cared. Give me
             the loveliest knight of limbs and hands,
             the magic and the trees whistling

in a first shedding of leaves. An
his sword be drawn, an I kneel naked
by the bed, and I have given
all a girl in such a time
             can give:

                   give it me again.

       Arthur

                   was the price, and the winning,
                   cause and ally of a fisher-king,

my father: in the smoke
from fired palaces, in the rushlit rooms
of my childhood,
                   the waste land;[36]

             what leprous issuings, what pustules and boils
             crawled on his thigh, my nurse

would gleefully retell, forgetting only
the red heart of the wound, the gouge
that raked from pelvis bone to knee, the which
I swabbed each night,

             each bitter night since I was ten. ·

       The torches smouldered. The cloths
       grew bloody and stank: some nights

36. My parents moved there in the mid-1970s, knocking through four feet of wall to
build a new room – which became the bedroom I shared with my brother – on top
of the kitchen. Later my father built a model railway to run around the edges of the
room, with a tunnel behind the radiator and a drawbridge to carry the trains over the
doorway. In the village shops closed, and stayed closed.

I thank my saviour I was ruined
                              when I was.

            Never forget

that Britain is a land of tides: in sweet, bucolic Arfon,
            Aeron, Elfed, in Ceredigiawn, the rustlings
                        of leviathan are heard,

and always the far-off lull of wave breaking
on wave will call the freemen

                        to a king's war.

                              So Arthur

                  was our hero, and only he
                  skirting the waves, tide-rips
                  and the swell could make

            that vessel, the one true bountiful cup,

            one and a piece with his own frozen shell.
                  The truth to tell,

I was his instrument, like so many others married,
gat on, dressed and mob-capped, accorded only

            the saving grace

of adjacent effigy, quarterly arms,
            the annexation to another's prayers; but all I wanted

I so briefly had.[37] Arthur,

37. My parents were not rich then. I can remember my father on his bike some way
down the tree-lined tunnel of a canal towpath, where he must have been cycling from
work in Swansea; I must have been watching for him in the old Morris Minor that my
mother drove, because I can picture her frowning with impatience. I think he was late,
and my mother had been waiting.

I have lost it all again. My womb
which was your making and undoing,

        made out in cast or beaten bronze,
        sieved for its issue, or prophecy
    where politic will dress as generation,
    nation as beast, hero in inflection,

Tara as Sarras, Drogheda
as Zion on its rock-bound hill,
heroic butchery
        as crusading zeal −

− my womb broke him, though I never could,
    to spite your kin who would not wear such clothes.

    Fierce wars and faithful loves
    though spread through three or surely four
        kingdoms
    could make no moral of my life,[38]

I who wanted him, the adulterer, would spite
    you, Arthur, and your queen,
    would drive him naked
    into the green crumbling land
    just to have him once.

Arthur,
    though your heart is broken
    remember me, if only
    for the stainless knight

---

38. In the end it was my grandparents who paid for the bulk of my education. I think
money worried my parents, and I can remember their disagreement but not their
words. I remember our being lost on the way somewhere, with the car stopped on a
small road between arched trees and hedges, a view over fields on our right and my
parents arguing; my mother mentioned my father's dad dying only that once. The way
she said it seemed angry. Did she mean for it to hurt?

I bore over the cusp
of the dark
                    into the world's sea.

Arthur,
         though there was
         no Britain for lovers,
         think kindly on us

when the weathers bear autumn
on golden breath, when the land
wasted with wars breaks:

         in your proud hands, Arthur,
         I am delivered. Do not
                    abandon me.

Explicit secunda pars.

Part III

10. Galaad

The harvest is blood. The cross
sticks in the craw. Christ in his hurt droops
languishing over the world.

Through park gates, among displaced
and half-demolished villages
I steered my horse
down fire-hung lanes. I was

the knight of gales, the hammer
of our Lord beating
        out a domed sky, a stretched sail,
        a beach and sands reaching away

to distant mountains, which echoing the sea say
                Acre, Antioch, Tyre.

And nearer, with smoke blown in
from the galleys, and the turk – the sand
sweeps to the salt air. Meek

as a lamb, holy
as a child still my vessel carves
shore to blood-lapped shore

        through the rain, and thunder's shadows.

                         Arthur,
I leave my father mute as a ghost, [39]

        I swim with blessed sail
        to your glory and my hereafter:

39. Many things can be traced back to Brecon: my great-great grandfather, John Davies, was JP there in the tail-end of the nineteenth century; my grandfather's mother was his daughter, now remembered as the stern, unbending, principled woman she became; and rightly so. She was among the founding members of the Labour movement, a campaigner for women's rights. Or so I am told.

what I did, beyond the shores of daylight
with Christ's pain ringing in the whorls
            of my skull

there was no undoing. That trespassing sire of mine?[40]

He brang coles in a bucket. An't please you sir,
he brake his leg. By the sullen hearth
            of Gwydir, tippling his seidr

from Jacobite glassware (Arthur you were ever

            the king over the water, as the barge turned slowly
                        to white spaces
            beyond Barra and all Uists).

What I did, among Cheviot and Blackface,
emptying saddles and sieges, laying the worldly low,

            made Arthur weep
            for his country
            and his foundered knights:
            autumn my season
            of sifting and scourge.

In their vowels and North-Sea-orientated argot
I heard them, without the doors;

            as I hear you, Lord, fettling your sickle
                        for the work t'morn. Wind blazes
                        from all corners of the sky. Elfed
                        in its poor upland blustered

in tide-patterns, in waves of wheat and grass. Soon
to the stubble, Lord, your instruments will come.

---

40. Our branch of that family, his first wife's, was passed over in John Davies' will in
favour of his third and last wife; the house that was given to her still stands on the hill
overlooking the canal and, further away, the wide curve of the Usk. Every so often my
mother, or my grandmother, will mention it as we pass.

What shrift I made, in that chapel beyond the rack
of surf, in the chambered mounds where God grows
shootlike into the world; you know well.

There I drank from the cup; its cold light a visitation
where I heard the voice of pride, and intercession
                              in the divine.

            No other could win it
                        but Arthur. Truth,

                  I was his agent,
      Arthur grown in ivy-coils, setting his roots
      deep in the boles of every hero since,
                  drawing them into his own orbit

                        of allegories, of lances
                  smiting sin's medusa, monopeds
                  and giants pressing in from recessed windows,
                        the night's sea-shadows.

      Arthur,
                  it was the world,

            your own table coloured with the rubric
                  of a mappa mundi. The blood
                        in rivers watering Eden.

      And riding against it, unconfessed,
      brought out of the hard years with their
                  half-understood names,

                        your knights died.

      Owain and Glewlwyd, you knights of Catraeth,
                  the sea closes over you with the storm loud
                        as a memory of saints.

Enough of that. I will tell you
of Britain, [41] as it stood
in the years after I came
before the face of God;

bloody with autumn, rich
with spilt gore and whitewashed chancels,
of great estate. It was decided

      between factions. It was Mordred
      gathering in pottery-smoke, in the ash
         of backyard forges, his army
         of chain-makers, weavers, nailers lifting
      their thankless hammers

to the hate of Arthur. Christ twisted
      bronze-forged upon Calvary
            weighs down

as increase from the iron hills. Christ in his hurt
smoulders for wrecked groves,
the streams of Glyn Nedd[42] soured
      and bright with mineral hues.

            I was the blaze and threshing flail
            rieving up all fellowship
            with briar hedges, with thorn
            and ash spears: forest and assart,

    Arthur abides not
    by the commons. The fire
    that cleaned Cranmer – divisions,
        contractions – relishes me.

41. When I am able, I drive my grandmother out into the countryside that she moved
to Brecon to enjoy; to the views of Tor-y-Foel from the saddle in the hills above Tal-
y-Bont reservoir, or the carefully-hidden valley where Sarn Helen climbs up from
Ystradfellte.
42. It is often this time of year that reminds me of the obscure beauty-spots of Powys,
and of driving my grandmother to see them down the leaf-covered minor roads that
climb around and over the wooded hills between their high, wet hedges.

                          Stand, then:
            for I am witness to the living word,

      its meanings, conformity
      and situations. I am
  ,   the cipher of my Lord.

                    Arthur,

            you knew who could be saved
                  and who must perish,

            what arks might, steered
            by prayer's soundings hove
                    to that far shore: I see you still,

                  tending your boat
            between a dark sea and heaven, behind you
            a flotilla of lights, your bright
            kind boys; shorn of the world

            and all cares, borne up
            by the soul's weight with you. Arthur,

      commend me to them,
      as I have them to God; even as war
            breaks the soil open
            with its roots. Arthur

      I did not mean to leave your darling-ones
      as harvest. Christ in his hurt mends [43]
      but slowly. The cross sticks
                        in the craw.

43. It is now almost two years since my grandfather died. Bereavement – my mother's,
my grandmother's – does not, after all, end in a flash of recognition. It dims into a back-
ground noise, a low, sad phonograph sound we can still hear.

11. Melwas

The white queen runs red
come autumn's end.[44] The valleys sing hymns
of preservation tight-mouthed;
over the breakfast table equally
rapt with a new *Archaeologia Cambrensis*
and fearing the sea-peoples – are they

                                  coming or going?

– as Arthur steers his *Mimosa* out
        between rising squalls. Yes, Arthur

                was my dupe,

            my unlikely gull, spritsail opening,
             riddling his grey feathers
      back into a dream

    of sea-flight; into the far oceans
     of the heart;
               bumbling, regal;
               mighty and inept. His queen

     I loved. She likewise, feeling the Trevivian copper
     of my limbs, hating the old prison

of her adultery, the slow ache
of language ebbing to those same
oceans; following Arthur, she said.   (*O éalaigh liom* –
                 the sense fails me.
                    & she will not come)

     In my glass palace, its marbles and park-gates
     laid under living elms,   she was happy.

---

44. When I was young my father kept sheep in our one-acre field, never more than two dozen at a time. Our oldest ewe, Lacey, who lived to be almost twenty – if I remember rightly – was buried at the bottom of the garden, under a few crab-apple trees.

Gwenhwyfar, feeling the shift
        of beam-engines, slate-cutters;[45]
so like the sea.

        Where was Arthur? The same knock
sounding him out as the hill groaned – at Penwyllt, Pwll Byfre,
at Craig-y-Dinas, sounding
even as in sleep he voyaged
                on a hero's wind.

Touching him, she told me,
        was cold, the deep cold
of echoes and glass; the bride-bed
                always strewn with snow. I
                warmed like a furnace fire
                she said.   (*Mo ghile mear* –
                        gone by barge,
                        or Cunard, or White Star)
Yet
                as she turned from the lancet, the light
                        that broke in from the garden – its
                        undergrown lawn, its empty bowers –
could show how old,
                how lined her face,
how the words like white hairs streaked
her simple, sad mouth:
                        ffarwel, she said,
                and the whitewash brushed over her.

What little I remember,
                        after, among the terraces
                where the unnamed one howled 'yield
                thou traitor knight', before the fine
                censorious meeting-houses;
                        where I trapped him in the deep measures
                at Blaenafon, at Wakefield and Standburn:

45. In the early nineties there were still a few small drift mines working on the Gwrhyd, the hill behind my parents' house. I remember seeing the small space of cleared, blackened ground with the hole leading into the hill, thick yellow and black armoured cabling spilling down out of sight. I did not think of it when I was young, but the whole hill is plainly marked with old drifts and spoil-heaps from almost three centuries of mining.

& his kin nis nohow where he was. After
     he had risen
     to the shadowed surface
     of the hills, after

     he had broken me
     on the rails, on the steam-ship plating:

for the last time, I saw Arthur. Vision
     and threat of vision.
     Cold iris. Islands

of a blue light where, if I had looked
          one moment longer I

would have been sailing, as he

sailed once in grail-voyage downstairs

to the singing kettle, the embers

of last night's hearth

fragments
         of a once-real sea. [46]

But I could not, and the life
heaved from my lungs. It was winter

     and the villages smoked like gledes
     in early frost. Gwalchmei pressed

his secrets to Arthur's ear, Mordred wept
     in the night, when no-one
       would hear

---

46. In my primary school we were read stories of miners and miner's children; we were taught about the different types of pit, from the bell-pit to the deep mine. But the miners were long gone from our village by then, leaving a handful of ageing men with some small compensation for their permanent, incurable lung diseases.

and the nameless one parted
from his Guenevere,
                              at last.

So near the end, Arthur

                    bloomed like a sick flower,
              opening only to weak sun
              on the winter sea. Britain,

quiescent, drowsy with conquest,
lulled with its fables of knights and shires

slept out the last loves
of a wounded land; touched up
its empire villas
                    with Mughal silver,[47]
calling lascar johnny to the cold
of Tyneside, past the rock of Alt Clud;

                    where Logris faced the sea, and a crossing
                    into legend. Even with wounds

as deep, I crossed. I saw the others
crossing before.
                              The sky
darkened ahead: smoke hung
on Arfon behind. In the night

there was a storm, a great gale
that separated us: and while it blew
I dreamed that Mordred came

47. They still opencast for coal right by our village, and at Brynhenllys a few miles from
our hourse. I cannot tell if summer rain dirty with coal-dust and a hole in the hill a
mile long is a fair exchange for thirty livings. Perhaps that is not the point. Memory is
not always convenient; for just as my grandfather was born in the industrial hinterlands
of Wales, so in searching for a backdrop against which the man stands clearly I find
myself touching the deeper legends of coal and steel, the ties between a centuries-dead
ironmaster and a life that I saw being lived.

felling the park-elms
and iron gates; swathing
walled gardens with a lance
of frost.

              Gwenhwyfar, Arthur,
I will never see Logris more,[48]
neither its tides nor winds: as the backwash hauls
                             over lost shores.

48. Perhaps only the shape of it is important, after all. It is true that I have tried to make a testament to all the people who have given the myth its force; but there are thousands more to whom I cannot give shape in my thoughts, and who can only be recognised by you who read this. I am limited by the scope of my own memories, but in relating them to you I hope that their form, if not their content, will make the myth give up its dead.

12. Le chevalier mal fet

He coughs up blood.
She sleeps alone:
dreams of the fire,
the love that melts bone[49]

    to blackened bone.

He hardly sleeps
for black spots on the lung:
closes his eyes
against the gaslight;

    against the done, and the undone.

At eight: "tea, dear?"
He will not answer them.
She pictures her husband
as she struggles with the stove:

    the fire again. His skin blisters in love,

for days too weak to rise.
At night his wounds break
their sutures; she launders
linen sheets with lye:

    defeated, pegs them on the line

with faint red-brown marks
that freeze in the winter air,
the house too big
and empty to be home.

49. You see it is sometimes hard to reconcile my memories of my grandfather with the man he clearly was, in his stories and memories of himself. It is quite hard to picture him as a boy at Cyfartha school, the converted gothic mansion of the Crawshays, struggling with geometry and music; much as with dreams, my recollections do not quite add up to a complete person.

Arthur passes
each night at ten. Sometimes stands outside:
watches the servant dousing lights
from room to room. Sometimes he disappears
back into smog,

to the moss-grown, ruinous
company, where seats
still blazoned for the long-
and newly-dead

watch. Mordred

of nights creeps in   (weary of agitation,
to slump upon the throne,   schooled
imagines a crown   in broadside printing,
of iron on his head,   speechmaking, dynamiting)

one riveted to the skull.

And the ill-made knight says:
Gareth, where are you? Gwalchmei
forgive me. He hears
the sullen pounding
of the sea

breaking on headland-forts,[50]
the fizz of searchlights
scouring gloomy reefs:

the channel echoes
to a shudder of guns; the love that is done

and wishes itself undone.

50. Perhaps memory in adversity retrenches itself; my grandfather loved Weston-Super-Mare because he had been happy there as a boy. Perhaps in the legend he is still crossing the Severn Sea on the Campbell sailings from Swansea, past Palmerston's defences on Brean Down and Lavernock, through Marconi's broadcasts, to Birnbeck island with its rusting, empty pier.

Arthur still broadcasts:
        "peace in our time,"
        with Mordred's divisions massing
        on the Ebro. The last best knight

forces down cold bacon,
a little soup. She feels her back
stiffen from stooping at the floors;
        feels her hair whiten. Arthur

propped up in bed sails
on radio waves to the shores
of a lost land:[51] the summer
        which in winter's country lives

        pressed into sepia,
        in the heart of Arthur
            a kind of Britain

with its bicycles clacking
down the lanes to Logris
        and Lyonesse that drifts

hourly out of reach. Arthur:

his paradox to be water
and vessel, the voyager plumbing

those dark, unreachable years.
Let them stay out of reach
            says Gwenhwyfar.

51. Or perhaps memory is that distant country that recedes from sight in every rear-view mirror, where the mind performs its obscure arithmetic to place my grandfather beside himself, here picnicking upon the Blorenge in South Wales, here looking out from a hotel dinner-table over the sea to the same country's coast; here talking about watching cowboy films as a boy, and here watching them. If you ask me who my grandfather was, could I find the words to answer you?

But the waves will not leave them alone,
any of them, brushing the stratosphere
          with their rumours; deployments,

          troop dispositions. Arthur casting his grief

     on shadowed Europe breaks nightly
          into static, calling his queen

          from Leningrad, Danzig,
          Tel Aviv, Minsk. She will not come,

thinks of the murdered one
whose blood tied Briton

to Briton; which now clots earth to earth:

for you will know the truth.[52]

          I

               was that knight, the ugly,
          the ill-made. It is hard
          to admit

               that I was there, wearing his skin. Hard
          to admit I loved my king

               and Guinevere both, and in my love
                    I ruined Britain, man and realm.

     Arthur, I will not ask;
     nor could you give.

52. Who were they? Who were they all, these people who are so alive in my memory
and in my imagination? And is it their country as well as mine, this patchwork land
that is forever slipping in and out of time and place?

But if there is
       some make-believe country –
       maybe named Logris –
where two people

who are older
than they dare recall
       can live, outside of love
       or fellowship, or time,

close only to each other
       and the sea: [53]

let them be there,
she turning her head
to a fair wind,

he holding her hand.
Let them go, Arthur,
as cleanly as Adam through Eden.

   Agnus,
              miserere.

The streetlights bend their heads in prayer.

53. Because time is short. To know a story, somebody first must tell it to you. When I had the chance to reckon up my grandfather's memories from his own telling, I did not take it, so instead I must listen for him here, over the background roar of the myth.

13. Medraut

Drums,

flutes.

I am sick of memories. I will wash it
     all away – haul
             away boys; mud
               on the deadman's faces mud
          on the sunk shields and helms, lobster-
     tail and all awash;

I will wash: bight by bight. Death may find you
on a clear day, beside the great water.

It is winter and the sun
rises shear over the world's
     shield-rim. To hear the murmur
     of the cannonade, the shouts and ruin[54]

of a united people – as God

ancient and haggard
looks away. All the rivers of Europe, spring and pool,

     Dnieper Elbe and Danube
     Vltava Hafren Siloah Euphrates where
my mind wanders my heart my heart.

The light is thicker than the river: Christ
     the Emperor

unrisen lies   his palms open springing

---

54. Sometimes that noise deafens us. Our memories become a small flicker against the
white noise that is thousands of years of wishful, brilliant, heartbroken people straining
to make themselves heard; and the careful turning of our own selves to receive only
the signals near to us is overwhelmed by the unfelt richness that is history and tradi-
tion and so much more.

from them the five rivers
of Eden. I picture

the beaches & the winter hills Powys Deheubarth Morgannwg
the machair sands their swallowed lives stranded house hearths
& the fire-place. The glow sinking into ash.

Elfed Aeron Rheged – edges
without places in them. Meanings aground
where whole seas retreated. The enemy

presses; all the sayings of you
are a battleground
I against Arthur – stranger   foreigner, in your blood –

& we divide the world.
Moon bloody rising. Sun dark eclipse.

A world, bounded. Arthur enmeshed
with kirtle seas. Afloat, the myth,
Britain   what   you will.

Prydwen the wisdom. Rhongomyniant
the killer. Caledfwlch the hard gap
of edge stinting on edge. Revelation: its threat

a ringing in your ears. Logris,
Lyonesse. I await the flood.

Arfderydd, Coed Celyddon, Baddon: I am resigned
to your grace and curses, Sulis Minerva. Mithras

in his souterrain wakes. Memory
looks at the faces
under the cauldron-lip. Water:
surface.

A ring of grotesques leering
a chase   a boar
a dragon at bay.

The steel drives

home.

Arthur, my heart.

I have lost him.
You shall have trees
that flourish green in one minute and are

fire-blooms the next; will see
prodigies born, gravity

and all its heavens silent
as moon   falls homeward howe-
ward
as the sun   grim cloud backing
lighting the course
of the land.

There Arthur fell, and Mordred was slain.

Once upon a
time

there were
two bodies
one in black,
the other in red-gold-green,
upon some other time
the red one stirred
the swells
blowing up from the sea
which one

was I? The story founders to its
end,
in sight of the waves

in the shallow water
its flotsam

                    of plastic
bottle-caps,
                    fishing floats,

                              where two armies on the shores
          of a legend had bled
                    once upon a
          time I think.

if I am watching this
                    I think the reception
          is grainy I cannot

                    make out the face

of the dead one? Is it

          the sound of drums,
          or waves. A sweet voice
          singing over water.[55]

          Arthur, too weak
          to rise in's harness
          sees at last

          the magic, and the sun-
          light falling between
          clouds. His sisters

          of the North,
          the small isles' daughters
          breaking the swell,

          & white hands reaching
          for him. I must
          look away, Arthur,

55. Sometimes, though, we are lucky, and the small voice that is the very real world
finds us; and we may find the lost, the marginal, the disappeared waiting for us in the
past's house. It may be that a history given is a worthless thing, but it is my heart's truth
that a history discovered is the only treasure I can possess.

when the dark barge comes,
              its sail

    set

for Uist Gwales Gwalia
                    my gwalia – graveyard
        of west-driven cultures. Tide-mark

at Europe's end. I must look away
            when their houses
are scattering white stones, Arthur;
            when the dark barge comes.

    The dark barge comes.

Epilogue: Morgana

One we lifted
and one we left, bleeding
his thankless life
        into the tide. We turned the boat

westward, into the light and storms.

Arthur, piece by piece
        in that long voyage
        you were disarmed.

First came the crown, its vapour
        of arms and assumed
            dignities:

                amherawdwr, *rex britannia,*

they shone and glittered
like shoals   as we dropped them
        over the side.

Next came his harness: I myself took
        Caledfwlch his great edge,

        quenched it in rough silk and let it cleave
            the waters; we undid each buckle,
                each trembling rivet of him as the whales
                    bucked, spouting
            in the luminous dark
            of that ocean. His mail heaved with a great splash
                and was gone.
Lighter now, the boat lifted on its one
        strung sail, skimming the crests
        as we took Arthur
                from his courtly robes.

Fine silks, satins, ermines, they spread
        behind us as a radiant wake,
        and the stars climbed towards the axis of the sky.

We took his naked body and washed it
in the salt spray; we might have healed that,
          were it not too late for any of my crafts

          but this: unstitching
the image of him, the old king
stalwart, bearded   royal even in death

we let it catch the wind,
the very shape of him thinning
like smoke
          until it was a flock of gulls
                    clouding our horizon. The night blew on

          heavy with rain. The stars vanished from view.

By many-coloured lamps we watched
the thing – not quite a man –
          that waited on the silks, the blazing outline

of a boy, that twitched
through youth to dotage as you turned
          your head. His smile was living

but cold. Strange lights blossomed
          in his sleeping shape.
We sailed straight
          on into the storm's mouth. Rain-blackened reefs
          streamed past: as we, so patiently

teased out the parts of him we knew.

          Pride, and greed
          for power, those bloated cankerous
                    organs we found

          to have grown around one stain,
                    one flaw,

          as pearls inside a shell. All that remained

was Arthur, his story: from boy
in a magician's tutelage

to king of an Atlantic colloquy
of isles: which has been

elsewhere rehearsed; and more, the million stories
he had drawn to him   flickered and spun
in his glass heart. Which broke

as we stood watching, pierced as it was
with Mordred's blade.

After a while, the lightning passed
the rain slackened

to a mist which lightened in the east.

We saw land's shadow and we thanked our God.

And so it seemed
that Arthur had died
before he reached
the very fringe
of daylight
& the land of apples. Britain
died with him.

And yet.

We made to move the body from the boat,

over the sands   shouldered
to the cairns that watched the bay. But it was

marvellous
>how light it felt, how slowly

in the new year's morning
>it dissolved, proving the story
>true. We wrote
>>no *HIC IACIT*,   we lit no fires,

thinking of empty armours   that lay
>under the sea. Arthur broken

>particulate hovered toward sunrise   like dew,
>>raining on Logris finely,
>>>>settling
in the small, the unexpected marks
of Britain. Arthur the green
>blade slashing midwinter sun

beginning as root, as tree, as boy — at least
I would prefer to think so:
>where he belongs, so that hills

may have a hero sleeping under them,
a voyager   & vessel of tales;

>such was my brother,
>>Arthur   who
scattering into the ocean's land left only

>an outline,
indistinctly
>as though eased of a great burden
>>>a figure

climbing the shores of dawn.[56]

---

56. As I say, my grandfather died on the 18th of February, 2008; but he was born in April, 1914, on the very edge of the First World War — by which I mean, the root that grows through him to me there meets other roots, which meet other roots beyond — by which I mean too, that he still flourishes forwards, into the newest instant of time. *Requiescat in pace*, you boy, you father, grandfather. And be thou with me.